BEST MALE GYMNASTS OF ALL TIME

BY BLYTHE LAWRENCE

SportsZone
An Imprint of Abdo Publishing
abdobooks.com

abdobooks.com

Published by Abdo Publishing, a division of ABDO, PO Box 398166, Minneapolis, Minnesota 55439.

Printed in the United States of America, North Mankato, Minnesota
042020
092020

Cover Photo: Amy Sanderson/ZUMA Wire/Cal Sport Media/AP Images
Interior Photos: Andy Buchanan/AFP/Getty Images, 5; Tatyana Zenkovich/EPA/Shutterstock/Rex Features, 7; Ben Stansall/AFP/Getty Images, 8; von der Becke/ullstein bild/Getty Images, 11; S&G/PA Images Archive/Getty Images, 12; AP Images, 14, 27, 28; Santiago Lyon/AP/Shutterstock/Rex Features, 17, 19; Craig Fujii/AP Images, 20; Amy Sancetta/AP/Shutterstock/Rex Features, 22–23; B. East/AP Images, 25

Editor: Charly Haley
Series Designer: Megan Ellis

Library of Congress Control Number: 2019954394

Publisher's Cataloging-in-Publication Data

Names: Lawrence, Blythe, author.
Title: Best male gymnasts of all time / by Blythe Lawrence
Description: Minneapolis, Minnesota : Abdo Publishing, 2021 | Series: Gymnastics zone | Includes online resources and index.
Identifiers: ISBN 9781532192357 (lib. bdg.) | ISBN 9781098210250 (ebook)
Subjects: LCSH: Gymnastics--Juvenile literature. | Gymnastics for men--Juvenile literature. | Sports--History--Juvenile literature. | Gymnastics for children--Juvenile literature.
Classification: DDC 796.44--dc23

CONTENTS

CHAPTER 1

THE GREATEST OF ALL TIME

As he reached to grasp the bar, Kohei Uchimura's face looked deep in concentration. One event remained in the men's all-around final at the 2016 Olympic Games in Rio de Janeiro, Brazil. The Japanese star was having a good competition, but he was still nearly a point behind Oleg Verniaiev of Ukraine. To overtake his main rival, Uchimura needed an excellent routine on the high bar.

Kohei Uchimura competes on the high bar.

267

The crowd inside the arena fell silent as Uchimura stepped up to perform. Four years earlier, Uchimura had been crowned Olympic champion. Could he repeat that now?

Uchimura didn't hesitate. One after another, he performed high-flying release skills. He let go of the bar and caught it again perfectly several times. When he cast into his double-twisting, double-layout dismount, time seemed to stand still. Uchimura soared through the air, twisting and turning. His feet hit the mat, and he stuck the landing flawlessly.

GREATEST OF ALL TIME

Afterward Uchimura paced the sidelines and waited for his score from the judges. Before these Olympics, many people had already called him the greatest male gymnast of all time. Had he done enough to win Olympic gold again? When his score came up, Uchimura took over the lead. But Verniaiev still had to perform.

Oleg Verniaiev won a gold medal for his performance on the parallel bars in the 2016 Olympics.

The Ukranian's high bar routine was one of the best of his career. It was clean and smooth. But Verniaiev did not take the same risks as Uchimura. He did not attempt any of the high-flying release moves Uchimura had done.

Uchimura, *left*, and Verniaiev celebrate their Olympic accomplishments.

That helped make the difference. The judges' scores put Verniaiev in second place. Uchimura had won his second Olympic gold medal! Verniaiev won the silver. Their duel was one of the greatest of the Olympic Games.

After the competition, Verniaiev praised Uchimura. He said he was happy to make the champion work hard for his title. He also likened Uchimura to Michael Phelps, the history-making swimmer who won his 23rd gold medal at the Rio Olympic Games.

Kohei Uchimura's incredible results are one reason why he is called the "GOAT" (greatest of all time) in men's gymnastics. But many other greats came before him. Like Uchimura, these gymnasts were talented and very determined. They overcame their own challenges in order to rise to the top of their sport. Their stories stretch all the way back to the early era of modern gymnastics.

CHAPTER 2

THE MAN OF IRON

Boris Shakhlin had the gift of being able to concentrate on his routines. He rarely made mistakes. Shakhlin made the hard moves he was performing look easy. When he performed on the still rings or high bar, he was able to keep his face perfectly calm. People admired this almost as much as they admired his technical skill.

Shakhlin did not have an easy childhood. He was born in Siberia, a region famous for long, cold winters. His mother died when he was

Boris Shakhlin competes on the rings in 1962.

CSV
JUG
GB
ITA
SPA
FRA

Shakhlin shows his skills on the parallel bars during an international sports festival in 1965.

very young, and his father died when Shakhlin was 12. It was the same year that Shakhlin had started practicing gymnastics. Shakhlin went to live with his grandmother, but he continued his gymnastics training. He kept getting better at it. In 1951 when Shakhlin was 19, he went to a prestigious gymnastics school in Kiev, Ukraine.

There he met Viktor Chukarin. Chukarin was older than Shakhlin and was one of the best gymnasts on the Soviet Union's team. Chukarin's focus and determination inspired Shakhlin to work harder at his own training.

Five years later, Shakhlin was selected as part of the Soviet team at the 1956 Olympic Games in Melbourne, Australia. Chukarin won the all-around gold and four other medals, while

VIKTOR CHUKARIN

Like Boris Shakhlin, Viktor Chukarin overcame extreme hardships early in life. He joined the Soviet Army and was taken prisoner during World War II (1939–1945). He spent four years in a concentration camp, a place where prisoners are forced to work during war. When Chukarin finally returned home to Ukraine after the war, he was so thin and weak that his own mother did not recognize him. Practicing gymnastics helped Chukarin regain his strength. He went on to win the all-around title at the 1952 and 1956 Olympic Games.

Shakhlin won a gold of his own on pommel horse. Chukarin retired from gymnastics after that Olympics. Shakhlin decided to continue.

In 1960 Shakhlin's hard work paid off. At the Rome Olympic Games, he won the all-around title and gold medals on the pommel horse, parallel bars, and vault. He was the

Shakhlin delivered a gold medal performance on the high bar in the 1964 Olympics.

only athlete at the Olympics that year to win four gold medals.

REFUSING TO GIVE UP

The high bar was perhaps Shakhlin's most impressive performance. His hand grip, a piece of equipment that protects the gymnast's hand as he swings around the bar, came off partway through his routine. Shakhlin refused to ruin his chance to win a medal by jumping down. Gripping the bar with just his bare hand, he continued. Doing the routine without the grip caused his hand to bleed. He finished anyway.

Winning the bronze medal for that routine made Shakhlin very proud. He won another Olympic gold in the same event four years later in 1964. During his career, Shakhlin won 13 Olympic medals, seven of which were gold. What he is remembered for is how he refused to give up. For his accomplishments, Shakhlin was nicknamed "the Man of Iron." He lived up to it.

CHAPTER 3

THE MAN FROM MINSK

Vitaly Scherbo was no stranger to greatness. Early in his career, the gymnast from Minsk, Belarus, proved nearly unbeatable. But as he learned, success can mean different things. It can mean winning a gold medal. For Scherbo, it also meant making a comeback after a near tragedy.

Scherbo was a rebellious but talented teenager. At his first gymnastics World Championships in 1991 in Indianapolis, Indiana,

Vitaly Scherbo helped lead the Unified Team to gold in the 1992 Olympics in Barcelona, Spain.

he finished second place in the all-around. But he was angry. He had wanted first. He promised himself he would do better at his next big competition.

At the 1992 Olympic Games in Barcelona, Spain, Scherbo kept his promise to himself. He was an unstoppable force, performing one

DMITRI BILOZERCHEV

Dmitri Bilozerchev is a gymnast who made an incredible comeback after a devastating injury. Bilozerchev was just 16 when he won the World Championships all-around title in 1983. Two years later, he was badly injured in a car accident. Doctors considered amputating his leg. Then they realized he was a famous gymnast. They were able to save Bilozerchev's leg, but no one was sure he would be able to return to gymnastics. The recovery was long and difficult, but Bilozerchev never gave up. In 1987 he was a world champion once more.

Scherbo, *center*, celebrates his victory in the individual all-around in Barcelona. His teammates placed second and third.

near-perfect routine after another. He won the gold medal in the all-around, along with an additional five gold medals for the team

Scherbo performs on the still rings.

competition and on pommel horse, still rings, vault, and parallel bars. No gymnast had ever won six gold medals in a single Olympic Games before. Scherbo became a legend overnight.

He continued to do well in gymnastics during the next few years. His life improved, too. Belarus was a hard place to live. So Sherbo, his wife Irina, and their baby daughter Kristina moved to Pennsylvania. Scherbo continued to train and compete well. He was ready to continue his golden streak at the 1996 Olympic Games in Atlanta, Georgia.

AN ACCIDENT

Seven months before the Olympics, Irina Scherbo was driving her car on an icy stretch of road. She lost control and crashed into a telephone pole. Irina was very seriously injured. Doctors were not sure whether she would live.

Irina was in a coma for weeks. Scherbo dropped everything to be by her side. He spent hours beside her hospital bed each day, praying she would wake up. Meanwhile, he had stopped training and fell out of shape.

A month after her accident, Irina finally woke up. She encouraged her husband to resume training for the Olympics. Inspired by her, Scherbo returned to the gym. He wanted to win more gold medals. He did not want them for himself, but for his wife.

Scherbo competes on pommel horse in 1996.

A COMEBACK IN ATLANTA

Scherbo returned to training. He was very focused. But he did not have enough time to fully prepare for the Olympics. In Atlanta he tried hard but did not manage to win any golds. He won four bronze medals. That gave him a total of 10 Olympic medals. He retired from gymnastics the next year. Scherbo may not have won the golds that he wanted so much in Atlanta. But his comeback is still recognized as an incredible achievement.

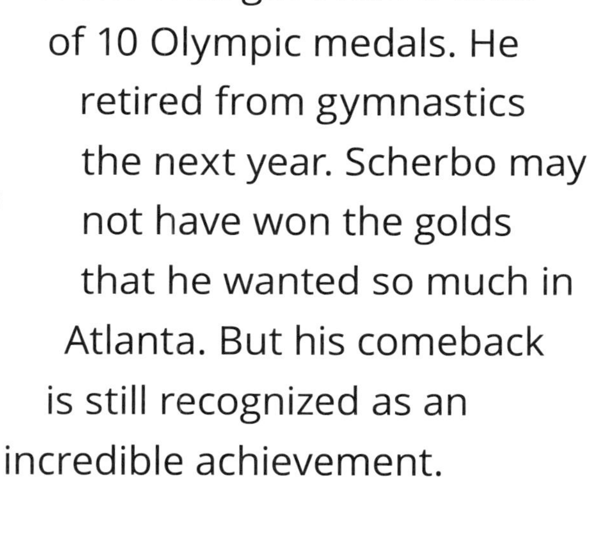

CHAPTER 4

THE MIRACLE ON MATS

Nobody believed it could happen. The US men's gymnastics team was strong. Maybe they could win bronze and a place on the podium at the 1984 Olympics in Los Angeles. But the team gold medal? No way.

Yet on a magical night at the Olympic Games, Team USA's Bart Conner, Tim Daggett, Jim Hartung, Scott Johnson, Mitch Gaylord, and Peter Vidmar surprised themselves and the world with their gold medal performance. Going into the

Mitch Gaylord was the first American gymnast to score a perfect 10 at the Olympics.

Olympics, the world champion Chinese team was favored to win the team title. The Japanese team was very strong as well. The talented Soviets would have had a great chance at taking the bronze medal, but the Soviet Union boycotted the Olympics that year for political reasons. That left the door open for another team to sneak onto the podium.

A CHANCE FOR TEAM USA

The Americans saw this opportunity in the team all-around competition. The United States had never won the team gold medal in men's gymnastics at the Olympics. The 1984 team hoped to be the first. Things went well from the beginning. After the first round of competition, the United States held the lead over China by a little more than one point.

The Chinese team fought back in the second and final round. Stars Li Ning and Tong Fei received multiple perfect scores. But the

Team USA pieced together multiple perfect performances in 1984, including Bart Conner's routine on parallel bars.

Team USA celebrates its gold medal.

Americans were just getting started. Vidmar nailed his routine on pommel horse and scored a perfect 10. Gaylord earned a perfect score on rings. Conner added a 10 on parallel bars.

Finally only high bar was left. In their corner of the arena, the Chinese gymnasts continued to put up big numbers. Gaylord, waiting to perform, had to make a choice. He usually did a very difficult release move, a double front flip over the bar. Gaylord wondered if he should play it safe and take the move out of his routine—but he decided to go for it. He caught the bar perfectly during the routine. The crowd cheered. Daggett followed up with a perfect 10, and Vidmar sealed the gold with an excellent routine of his own.

Conner, Daggett, Gaylord, Hartung, Johnson, and Vidmar were the first American men's team to win the Olympic title in gymnastics. Because it was unexpected, today the victory is remembered by some people as the "Miracle on Mats."

GLOSSARY

ALL-AROUND

When gymnasts compete in all of the events as an individual. The all-around champion earns the most points from all the events combined.

COMA

Being unconscious for a long time while the body heals itself from an injury.

DISMOUNT

To land after performing on the vault, pommel horse, balance beam, high bar, uneven bars, rings, or parallel bars.

PARALLEL BARS

An event where male gymnasts swing between two bars of equal height.

POMMEL HORSE

An event in which male gymnasts balance on their hands on a bench covered with foam, rubber, and leather that has two plastic handles on the top (the pommels).

RELEASE MOVE

A gymnastics move on horizontal bar where the gymnast lets go of the bar and then catches it again.

STILL RINGS

An event in which male gymnasts perform routines holding onto a pair of rings suspended above the ground.

VAULT

An event in which gymnasts push off a table and do flips and twists in the air.

MORE INFORMATION

BOOKS

Mattern, Joanne. *Simone Biles: America's Greatest Gymnast*. New York: Scholastic, Inc., 2018.

Nicks, Erin. *Best Female Gymnasts of All Time*. Minneapolis, MN: Abdo Publishing, 2020.

Schlegel, Elfi, and Claire Ross Dunn. *The Gymnastics Book: The Young Performer's Guide to Gymnastics*. New York: Firefly Books, 2018.

ONLINE RESOURCES

To learn more about the best male gymnasts of all time, please visit abdobooklinks.com or scan this QR code. These links are routinely monitored and updated to provide the most current information available.

INDEX

ABOUT THE AUTHOR

Blythe Lawrence is a journalist from Seattle, Washington.